APPLE
WATCH
USER GUIDE
FOR **NEWCOMERS**

The unofficial Apple Watch series 4 user manual for beginners and seniors

Stephen W. Rock

Dedicated to all my readers

Acknowledgement

Ii want to say a very big thank you to Michael Lime, a 3D builder, my colleague. He gave me moral support throughout the process of writing this book.

Table of Contents

Introduction

The title of this book already gives a hint on what the book is about. It is a guide for new users of Apple Watch series 4

The topics covered include Apple Watch tips and tricks, pairing Apple Watch with your iPhone, and maintenance tips for Apple Watch series

You'll be a pro in using Apple Pay. You'll be an iOS 12 pro. Yes, an iOS 12 pro.

Now, start savoring the content of this book.

Chapter 1

Getting Started With Your Apple Watch

Thee Apple watch is about the best watch you can ever have in this current age; at least for now. Who wouldn't be pleasured to own a little wrist device that's capable of helping with time tracking, fitness, message on the go, and much more? As a big fan of Apple, I took the time to see what's in the costly watch series. The Apple Watch Series 1 and 3 come with a casing which could be aluminium, steel, or ceramic. You'd also find strap, an AC power adapter, a magnetic inductive charger, and an introductory pamphlet.

The Apple Watch, in some ways, takes after the iPhone X's design. Both are all screen, have no home button, and both have impressive functionality for having relatively few physical buttons. Like the iPhone X, the Apple Watch has a side button, which is used to turn it on and off and do some other tricks and tasks. The Watch goes on to have a unique interface: The Digital Crown. When we combine all these with the multitouch screen's pressure-sensitive Force Touch capabilities, we simply agree that we've got a super-awesome, little wrist computer.

Setting Up Your Apple Watch From Scratch

No doubt, you need to set your Apple Watch so it can be fully ready for action. Setting up your smart watch isn't rocket science. It is so easy. So where do we start? Consider the following steps:

1. Once pairing process is complete, tap **Set up as new Apple Watch**
2. Tap either **left** or **right** to inform Apple Watch on which wrist you intend to wear the watch
3. Tap agree to confirm with the watch OS Terms and condition.
4. Tap agree for confirmation
5. Enter your apple ID to set up **Activation Lock** and **Find My iPhone**
6. Tap **Ok** to show you understand **Shared Settings** for iPhone and Apple watch
7. Tap create a pass code to create a pass code for apple watch (you can choose to add a long pass code or a short one by following prompt)
8. Tap enter your pass code and confirm
9. If you are using an Apple watch series 3 with LTE service, select whether to set up cellular on your Apple Watch
10. To indicate you understand emergency SOS tap **Continue on** your iPhone

11. Tap **Install All** to install all the watch OS apps are available on your iPhone
12. Give time for your apple watch to syncing with your iPhone
13. Your apple watch is ready to be use you can view basic navigation tips on your smart watch by tapping **Apple Watch Basics.**

Restoring Apple Watch from a back up

Once you are done pairing your apple watch with your iPhone tap **Restored from Backup** button note that before you can set up a new watch with Back on iOS 11, you will need to make a backup of your old watch on a device running iOS 11

✓ Choose the relevant backup and accept the terms and condition
✓ Follow prompts

Chapter 2

The Side Buttons

Now let's see how to use the side buttons.

On/Off

If your Apple Watch is on, press and hold the side button to access the power screen. Then simply slide the **Power Off** slider to turn the smart Watch off.

Enable Power Reserve Mode

- ✓ First, ensure your Apple Watch is displaying a watch face. Once this is seen, swipe up from the button of the screen to activate **Control Center**.
- ✓ Tap the Battery Percentage reading.
- ✓ Tap the Power **Reserve button** and then tap **Proceed**.

To exit Power Reserve Mode, simply press and hold on the Slide Button. Your Apple Watch will restart. So expect to wait between 30 seconds and 2 minutes depending on your model.

Reboot

You might ask, why rebooting? Yes, rebooting is a very old trick the troubleshooting book, and it works well on the Apple Watch. The following simple steps will help you reboot your computer watch:

- ✓ Press and hold down the side button until three horizontal sliders pop up.
- ✓ Drag the **Power Off** slider to the right (your Apple Watch must be disconnected from its charger to use the **Power Off** slider, else the slider is disabled).
- ✓ Press and hold down the slide button until the Apple logo shows up.

Reset Home Screen Layout

This is cool if you want to return your Apple Watch to factory default. This, however, cannot be done with the buttons on the Watch. You'd need the **Watch app** on your iPhone.

- ✓ Open the Watch app and tap the **My Watch** tab.
- ✓ Select **Reset**.
- ✓ Tap **Reset Home Screen Layout** .
- ✓ Tap **Reset Home Screen** to confirm your selection.

Reset Your iCloud Sync Data

This will be fine if you're having issues with calendar or contacts syncing properly. Once you reset, your Apple Watch's calendar and contacts will be replaced with the most recent iCloud sync from your iPhone.

- ✓ Open the Watch app and tap the **My Watch** tab.
- ✓ Select **Reset**.
- ✓ Tap **Reset Sync Data**.

Chapter 4

Apple Watch Tips And Tricks

Get Into The Control And Notification Center Easily

There was a time when the only way you could get into the Notification Center and Control Center was through the face screen of the watch. However with the recent watchOS you have the ability to access the Control Center and Notification Center from just about anywhere. With this, you can even access them from Third-party apps

What you do is put your finger at the top or bottom of the watch display. You should now see a piece of the Control Center or the notification center. Once it shows, you now have the ability to expand it to full display.

Say Bye To Walkie-Talkie

Any time you raise your wrist, there's a chance that you'll see a Walkie-Talkie icon that comes out at the top of the screen. If this is this case, then we could say that you've checked yourself in the Walkie-Talkie app as available.

If you would like to remove this relentless symbol,
1. Open up the **Walkie-Talkie app** on the Apple Watch
2. Then you go upwards to the top of contacts. You do this by using the digital crown of the watch.
3. Tap and turn off **Available**

Immobilize Notifications

There are things set by default on your watch. And one of them is the fact that your watch brings up the notifications from apps on your iPhone with alerts. At first you might think this is cool, but it might get old very fast.

To turn it off, just
1. Wait for the time you receive a notification from an app that you want to disable the notifications for.
2. When it shows up, slide left from it.
3. From here you should see three dots, select it
4. Choose **Turn Off On Apple watch**

This option to disable is really cool cause in previous watchOS, you would have to dig in your iPhone app and enter each app one by one to disable them.

Offline Podcast

Apple has finally launched the longed-for app for Podcasts. This is available in watchOS 5 and it allows you to use your iPhone to stream podcasts. You can do this with cellular data or Wi-Fi. Then you can be able to listen to them through headphones that are connected to Bluetooth

But something that is interesting is, with this Podcast app, you can sync and keep current podcasts for your iPhone straight to you Apple watch. With this you can now listen you them offline. To find the list of episodes, go to **Library** then select **Episodes**.

Use A Monogram

If you're one who uses the Infograph watch face or Color watch face then you would like to hear that you can now add a custom monogram. This can be used to form your initials, nickname and others.

If you would like to make your own monogram,
1. Open the **iPhone Watch App**
2. Choose **My Watch** tab
3. Hit **Clock**
4. Select **Monogram**

Include some letters in the field. With this, when next you choose the info graph watch face or Color watch face, you can select Monogram.

Tweak The Design Of The Control Center

With the watchOS 5 you can now change the buttons in the Control Center to the way you want. Previously, the Control center design was permanent.

To do this;
1. Enter the **Control Center** normally
2. Move to the bottom and chose **Edit**
3. To show that they are set for you to move them, the buttons should start to shake
4. Long press a button and move to the place it you want it to be

Connecting to a Wi-Fi

It has now been made possible to log in and browse Wi-Fi networks just from your own Apple watch. This feature is available on the watchOS 5. Previously, this was connected to the Wi-Fi of your iPhone.

To connect to a Wi-Fi network on your watch,
1. Enter the **Settings** app
2. Select **Wi-Fi**
3. From the list presented, choose a network that's available
4. From here you use the gesture input of the screen to enter the password

Include Cities In The Weather App.

Unlike any feature, the weather app has taken a complete overhaul in the watchOS 5 since the previous versions. When you select the radial forecast for one city, it will round up through chance of rain, temperature and other conditions

Now, when you scroll down with the help of the digital crown, you will be able to get extra information like the speed of the wind or the air quality.

Also, you can also add further forecasts for different locations in the world.

1. In the main screen, scroll to the bottom
2. Select **Add City**
3. You can state your preference or just jot down the city name

Force-Quit Stubborn Apps

If this hasn't happened to you yet then it might still happen in the future. Some apps will just crash and stop refreshing and receiving live data. With the watch face complications, this can happen too.

When this happens all you is force-quit the app in your watch. To do this;

1. With the app you want to force-quit, hold down the side button of you Apple Watch
2. When the power down menu shows up, release the side button.
3. Now, hold down the Digital Crown

The app should quit and come back to the home screen so you can open it again

Talk To Siri With No Buttons

With the new watchOS, watchOS 5, you now have the feature of speaking to Siri on your watch without pressing the Digital crown. This option is very easy to use, you can find it in Settings.

1. Go to **Settings**
2. Then **General**
3. Select **Siri**
4. Choose **Raise To Speak**

When you've enabled this feature, all you have to do next time you want to invoke Siri, is to just raise your hand to your mouth and start to talk Siri.

Hey you don't even have to say 'Hey Siri'. Just start speaking.

Alert For Running Pace

For runners, this is good news. Apple has now made it possible for your apple watch to enable pace alerts. With this you be able to test your capability to stick to the set pace.

When you want to track your run next time,
1. Enter the **Workout App**
2. Select the button with three dots.
3. Slide to the bottom and hit **Set Pace Alerts**.

You can choose to get alerts for you average pace after you complete a mile.

Do The Activity Challenge

You may be someone who shares his activity with friends who use Apple Watches. Now you can do a 7-day activity competition with them and challenge them for the chance to win an award

To do this;
1. Enter the **Activity App** on your watch
2. Slide to the Sharing screen
3. Select a friend
4. Move down to the bottom and press the button for **Invite**

The invitation for the competition will be sent and the receiver will be given a deadline of 48 hours to reply.

Switch To Grayscale

On the Apple watch Series 4, the infograph watch faces can be really colourful especially when you've crammed them with complications. While this might be cool for some, for others it's just too much color. If you find the colorful display a little too much, you can always switch to grayscale.

To switch on the display setting to grayscale in the Apple Watch,
1. Enter the **My Watch** tab
2. Go to **General**
3. Then **Accessibility**
4. From here, turn on the toggle for **Grayscale**.

Quietly Get Notifications

To access this feature, all you do is go back to the same menu for notification management that we mentioned earlier. After you enabled this option, you can still get notifications from the application in question. The only thing is that you don't receive alerts as they are being sent to your Apple Watch

Something you should keep in mind is that these changes will be effective on your iPhone too. So this means that when those apps send notifications, you will still get them in your notification center. But they won't be all up in your face and start appearing on the lock screen, showing as a banner or making noises.

Browse And Clear

Apple has included the ability to support WebKit in the watchOS 5. What this is trying to say is that you can open web links that are gotten in apps on your watch. Like the links you get in Messages or Mail. With is feature, those contents don't have to pass you by, you can view them right from your watch.

If you would like to keep your browsing record private, the watchOS 5 also has the alternative to sweep the browsing history and any trace that your watch viewed that content.

All you do is;
1. Go to **Settings**
2. Then **General**
3. Select **Website Data**
4. Choose **Clear Website Data**

Setting Alarm

When you hear the term 'set alarm' on your watch, it sounds pretty easy to do, it's a watch how hard can setting alarm be. If you thought that, you're right. Setting alarms on your Alarms on your apple watch is not that hard. You just tell Siri something like; 'Set an alarm for 5 am'

But there's much more to do than just setting alarms. Like how to use Nightstand mode or how to set alarms and keep them silent.

To setup nightstand mode;
1. Enter the **Settings**
2. Then **General**
3. Select **Nightstand mode**

How To Take A Screenshot.

On your Apple watch, taking a screenshot is pretty easy. Just press the Digital crown and Action button simultaneously. Once you do that the image will now be saved in your iPhone's camera roll

This simple step to take a screenshot however does not happen by default. You'll have to switch on this option yourself.

1. Got to the **Watch Companion app**
2. Then **General**
3. From here you will be able to turn on and turn off **Enable Screenshots**

Adding Music To Your Watch

With cellular support, Apple music streaming is available directly on the Apple Watch. You still have the option to add mp3 music and connect it to Air Pods

To enable this,
1. Go to the **Companion Watch App**
2. Enter the **Music** Section
3. From here you can choose from the option it gives

Those options are a lot easier than before when you had to first create a playlist before you can sync any music.

If you want to get the best of your music, you will want to pair it with Bluetooth headphones. The watch will even ask you to if you would like to sync to headphones.

Use Your Watch To Unlock Your Mac

If you have a Mac to match with your Apple Watch, you can leave out passwords and use your watch to unlock your Mac. Just be sure that your Mac is using macOS Sierra 10.12 and newer or mid-2013

To pair these two devices together, you want to ensure that they are signed into your own iCloud account.

1. Go to **System Preferences** in you Mac
2. Choose **Security and Privacy**
3. Press the **General** tab
4. From here, you'll be able to set your Mac to be unlock by you watch

Verify that two-factor authentication is enabled on your Mac.

Alter The Volume Of The Air Pods

You have you ask Siri if you want to change the volumes on your Air Pods and not bring out your iPhone,
If you're using an Apple watch too you can also do something like that.

If you're playing music on your watch and it uses watchOS 5, you can change the volume by turning the Digital Crown. This is way is also convenient.

Using The Flashlight

Apple watch has a built in flashlight. To use it, just swipe up to open the Control Center and Select the Flashlight. You also have the option to even switch the light modes from flashing white to plain white to emergency red.

Use Your iPhone To Answer Watch Calls

If you have your iPhone with you, you can receive calls with your watch. Just make sure not to talk for a long time with it.

Whenever you get a call, Scroll up select **Answer on iPhone**.

Setting Up And Pair Your Apple Watch With Your iPhone

The Apple Watch and iPhone are two wonderful devices that are both compatible and interesting to use. Pairing both devices isn't any difficult. I'm going to be explaining how to pair both devices in two alternatives; automatically and manually.

Pairing the Apple Watch and Phone automatically

Follow the under listed steps;

1. Launch the 'Watch app' on you iPhone or you can bring both the watch and iPhone close together to create a similar interface to the iPods pairing screen, which will then launch the Watch app.
2. Tap 'Start Pairing' and move your phone over your Apple Watch until the Watch is lined up in the center of the yellow rectangle.
3. When you see the message **Your Apple Watch Is Paired**, you can proceed with the next step.

4. Select whether to set up Apple Watch from scratch or to restore Apple Watch from backup.

Pairing the Apple Watch and iPhone manually

If you can't get your Apple Watch to pair with iPhone, the manual steps under-listed will be of great help to you. Instead of using the nifty QR-code-style process for pairing, you will use your Apple Watch's name.

1. Launch the **Watch app** on your iPhone device and tap **Start Pairing**
2. Tap **Pair Apple Watch Manually**.
3. On the Watch tap **i to** view the device's name.
4. On the iPhone, select your **Apple Watch** from the list.
5. Select whether to set up Apple Watch from scratch or to restore Apple Watch from backup.

How to Pair a new iPhone with an existing Apple Watch

You cannot manually make a backup of your Apple Watch to cloud. This is because backups are intrinsically tied only to your iPhone's Cloud or iTunes backups. As such, you have to manually un-pair your Apple Watch, which will then synchronize automatically its latest data to your iPhone backup.

How To Use Apple Pay On Your Apple Watch

As long as you are in the United States and have a supported credit or debit card, you can use Apple Pay on your Apple Watch. This chapter is dedicated to teaching you how.

Adding A Credit or Debit Card

The following steps will help you:

1. Launch the **Apple Watch app** on your iPhone and tap on **My Watch** in the bottom navigation.
2. Tap on **Passbook & Apple Pay**
3. Tap add **Credit or Debit Card** and tap **Next** in the upper right hand corner.
4. Enter the security code for the card you have on file with iTunes.
5. Tap **Next** in the upper right hand corner and agree to your cardholder's terms and conditions.

Once verification is complete, your card will show up in Apple Pay.

You can add more cards if you want. All you need do is follow the above protocols up till **Add Credit or Debit Card.** If you're having issues, tap **Add Card Details Manually** at the bottom.

- ✓ Fill in the necessary information and tap **Next** in the upper right hand corner.
- ✓ Repeat this process for every card you'd like to use for Apple Pay on your Apple Watch.

How to make payment with your Apple Watch and Apple Pay

Now that you have successfully added up your card details on Apple Pay, you want to start making payments for purchases not so? This process is quite straight-forward. Consider the following steps:

- ✓ At a pay point, double click the side button on your Apple Watch so your payment cards can pop up.
- ✓ Select the card you'd like to use by swiping from side to side.
- ✓ Position your Apple Watch towards the reader and wait until you feel a confirmation and hear a beep, meaning that your payment was proc4ssed.

How to remove a card from Apple Pay on Apple Watch

Removing a card from Apple Pay on you iPhone is not out especially when the card has expired. You could still leave old cards on Apple Pay but of what use will they be? The following steps will help you delete a card on your Apple Watch:

- ✓ Open the **Apple Watch app** on your iPhone and tap on **My Watch** in the bottom navigation.
- ✓ Tap **Passbook & Apple Pay**.
- ✓ Select the card you'd like to remove ad tap on **Remove Card**.
- ✓ Tap on **Remove** again to confirm.

Change The Size Of Texts

If you're one who strains to see what the notifications on the watch, you can just easily change the size of the texts.

To do this,

1. Go to **Settings**
2. Select **Brightness and Text Size**
3. Tweak it to how you see fit

Chapter 5

Basic Maintenance Tips For Your Apple Watch

No matter how useful your Apple Watch may be, if you don't take of it you are otherwise sayings it's useless and not important to you. The watch is expensive, take care of it. I have categorized caring for your Apple Watch into three subheadings. Now, let's take the first.

How to clean and dry Apple Watch

1. Turn off Apple Watch and disconnect from charger.
2. Wipe Apple Watch clean using a nonabrasive, lint-free cloth. You could use slightly wet cloth.
3. Dry Apple Watch with a nonabrasive lint-free cloth.

This cleaning exercise should be done once every two weeks to keep your Apple Watch glittering always like it was brand New.

How to clean and dry Apple Watch band

For leather bands

1. Using a nonabrasive, lint-free cloth, wipe the leather area of the band clean. If you want you could dampen the cloth lightly with fresh water.
2. Do not soak leather bands in water.
3. Dry leather bands thoroughly before attaching back to Apple Watch.
4. Do not expose leather bands to direct sunlight, at high temperatures, or in humidity.

For no-leather bands, simply clean with a nonabrasive, lint-free cloth slightly dampened in fresh water.

How to clean and dry the Digital Crown

Sometimes, the Digital Crown might get stuck because of debris. The follow cleaning procedures will solve the problem:

1. Turn off Apple Watch. Ensure it is disconnected from its charger.
2. If you have a leather band, remove it.
3. For 10 to 15 seconds, hold the Digital Crown under lightly running, warm, fresh water. Please do not use any soap or other cleaning products. Just water.
4. Make sure you continue to turn and press the Digital Crown as water runs over the gap between the housing and Crown.
5. Use a nonabrasive, lint-free cloth in drying your Apple Watch.

NOTE: if you have allergies, regularly clean your Apple Watch with fresh water only. For skin irritations that might surface, do not wear Watch too tight on your wrist. Allow room for your skin to breathe.

Disclaimer

In as much as the author believes beginners will find this book helpful in learning how to use the Apple Watch, it is only a small book. It should not be relied upon solely for all Apple Watch tricks and troubleshooting.

About the author

Stephen Rock has been a certified apps developer and tech researcher for more than12 years. Some of his 'how to' guides have appeared in a handful of international journals and tech blogs. He loves rabbits.

Facebook page @ Techgist